Copyright © 2011 XAMonline, Inc.

All rights reserved. No part of the material protected by this copyright notice may be reproduced or utilized in any form or by any means, electronic or mechanical, including photocopying, recording or by any information storage and retrievable system, without written permission from the copyright holder.

To obtain permission(s) to use the material from this work for any purpose including workshops or seminars, please submit a written request to:

XAMonline, Inc.
25 First Street, Suite 106
Cambridge, MA 02141
Toll Free: 1-800-509-4128
Email: info@xamonline.com
Web: www.xamonline.com
Fax: 1-617-583-5552

Library of Congress Cataloging-in-Publication Data

Wynne, Sharon A.
    PRAXIS Principles of Learning and Teaching (K-6) 0522 Practice Test 2:
Teacher Certification / Sharon A. Wynne. -1st ed.
    ISBN: 978-1-60787-130-9
    1. PRAXIS Principles of Learning and Teaching (K-6) 0522 Practice Test 2
    2. Study Guides   3. PRAXIS   4. Teachers' Certification & Licensure
    5. Careers

Disclaimer:

The opinions expressed in this publication are the sole works of XAMonline and were created independently from the National Education Association, Educational Testing Service, or any State Department of Education, National Evaluation Systems or other testing affiliates.

Between the time of publication and printing, state specific standards as well as testing formats and website information may change that is not included in part or in whole within this product. Sample test questions are developed by XAMonline and reflect similar content as on real tests; however, they are not former tests. XAMonline assembles content that aligns with state standards but makes no claims nor guarantees teacher candidates a passing score. Numerical scores are determined by testing companies such as NES or ETS and then are compared with individual state standards. A passing score varies from state to state.

Printed in the United States of America

PRAXIS Principles of Learning and Teaching (K-6) 0522 Practice Test 2
ISBN: 978-1-60787-130-9

Praxis Principles of Learning and Teaching (K-6) 0522
Post-Test Sample Questions

STUDENTS AS LEARNERS

1. Which of the following is not a stage in Piaget's theory of child development?
   (Average) (Skill 1.1)

   A. Sensory motor stage

   B. Pre-optimal stage

   C. Concrete operational

   D. Formal operational

2. It is essential that teachers develop relationships with their students and are aware of their personalities. Which of the following is an example of why this is important?
   (Easy) (Skill 2.2)

   A. Because most students do not have adult friends

   B. Because most teachers do not have friends who are children

   C. So that teachers can stay abreast of the social interaction between children

   D. Because, then teachers can immediately identify behavioral changes and get the child help

3. When students provide evidence of having special needs, standardized tests can be:
   (Rigorous) (Skill 2.4)

   A. Given out with the same predetermined questions as what is administered to students without special needs

   B. Exempted for certain children whose special-needs conditions would prevent them performing with any reliability or validity

   C. Administered over a lengthier test period (i.e. 4 hours instead of three or two)

   D. All of the above

4. Mrs. Grant is providing her students with many extrinsic motivators in order to increase their intrinsic motivation. Which of the following best explains this relationship?
(Rigorous) (Skill 3.2)

   A. This is a good relationship and will increase intrinsic motivation

   B. The relationship builds animosity between the teacher and the students

   C. Extrinsic motivation does not in itself help to build intrinsic motivation

   D. There is no place for extrinsic motivation in the classroom

5. A teacher's posture and movement affect the following student outcomes except:
(Easy) (Skill 3.3)

   A. Student learning

   B. Attitudes

   C. Motivation

   D. Physical development

6. In the classroom, the concept of management transition describes:
(Rigorous) (Skill 3.4)

   A. How the administration switches between the principal and vice principal

   B. How parents are prepared for when their children move from one grade to the next

   C. How students monitor the time they spend moving from class to class

   D. How teachers use time effectively so the class moves smoothly from one activity to another

7. A laminated seating chart can assist teachers in simplifying all of the following tasks except:
(Easy) (Skill 3.4)

   A. Performing self-assessments

   B. Taking attendance

   C. Making daily notes

   D. Keeping track of participation

INSTRUCTION AND ASSESSMENT

8. **What is the most important benefit of students developing critical thinking skills?**
   (Easy) (Skill 4.1)

   A. Students are able to apply knowledge to a specific subject area as well as other subject areas

   B. Students remember the information for testing purposes

   C. Students focus on a limited number of specific facts

   D. Students do not have to memorize the information for later recall

9. **This instructional strategy engages students in active discussion about issues and problems of practical application.**
   (Easy) (Skill 4.2)

   A. Case method

   B. Direct instruction

   C. Concept mapping

   D. Formative assessment

10. **Describe the difference between a LAN and a WAN?**
    (Average) (Skill 4.4)

    A. WANs allow computers to communicate over greater distances than LANs

    B. LANs allow computers to communicate over greater distances than WANs

    C. WANs and LANs provide the same geographical range

    D. WANs and LANs are both ineffective

11. **Two powerful internal factors influencing students' academic focus and success are their _____ and _____.**
    (Rigorous) (Skill 5.2)

    A. resources and class sizes

    B. parental involvement and teacher preparation

    C. efforts and academic outcomes

    D. attitudes and perceptions about learning

12. Which of the following test items is not objective?
    (Easy) (Skill 6.0)

    A. Multiple choice

    B. Essay

    C. Matching

    D. True/false

13. Of the following definitions, which best describes a standardized achievement test?
    (Rigorous) (Skill 6.1)

    A. It measures narrow skills and abilities

    B. It measures broad areas of knowledge

    C. It measures the ability to perform a task

    D. It measures performance related to specific, recently acquired information

14. It is most appropriate to use norm-referenced standardized tests for which of the following?
    (Average) (Skill 6.1)

    A. For comparison to the population on which the test was normed

    B. For teacher evaluation

    C. For evaluation of the administration

    D. For comparison to school on which the test was normed

15. What is the best example of a formative assessment?
    (Average) (Skill 6.2)

    A. The results of an intelligence test

    B. Correcting tests in small groups and immediately recording the grades

    C. An essay that receives teacher feedback and can be corrected by students prior to having a grade recorded

    D. Scheduling a discussion prior to the test

16. **This method tests the validity and reliability of a test by dividing a single test into two parts and comparing them.**
    (Easy) (Skill 6.3)

    A. Split-half

    B. Test-retest

    C. Equivalent forms

    D. Two-set

17. **An example of reliability in testing is ____**
    (Average) (Skill 6.3)

    A. Items on the test produce the same response each time

    B. The test was administered with poor lighting

    C. Items on the test measure what they should measure

    D. The test is too long for the time allotted

COMMUNICATION TECHNIQUES

18. **Outlines, graphs, and models are particularly good for which type of learners?**
    (Easy) (Skill 7.1)

    A. Auditory

    B. Kinestetic

    C. Visual

    D. Olfactory

19. **Which of the following is the best strategy to probe for student understanding of a specific topic?**
    (Rigorous) (Skill 9.1)

    A. Assigning writing exercises that are graded for correctness

    B. Allowing students to write on any topic

    C. Suggesting that students write in a journal that is checked at the end of the semester

    D. Assigning writing exercises that focus on recording students' thoughts on the topio

PROFESSION AND COMMUNITY

20. Ms. Jones has just read an article on an exciting new instructional strategy; she is considering incorporating this strategy in her classroom. As a research-oriented professional, what should be her next step? *(Rigorous) (Skill 10.2)*

    A. Read textbooks that deal with a wide range of theories

    B. Perform a literature search to see what else has been written on the topic

    C. Talk with other teachers about their opinions

    D. Begin incorporating the strategy with some students in the class

21. What is the most powerful benefit of teachers conducting frequent self-assessment? *(Average) (Skill 10.3)*

    A. They identify areas of weakness and seek professional development opportunities to strengthen them

    B. By observing their own teaching, teachers save themselves the pressure of being observed by others

    C. They also learn their strengths and reduce the time spent on areas not needing attention

    D. Their practice of self-reflection offers a model for students to adopt in self-improvement

22. Teachers must hold themselves to high standards. When they engage in negative actions such as fighting with students, they are violating all of the following except: *(Easy) (Skill 10.3)*

    A. Ethics

    B. Professionalism

    C. Morals

    D. Fiscal

23. **Often, schools and communities interact for the following activities except?**
(Average) (Skill 11.1)

    A. Blood drives

    B. Legal proceedings

    C. Meeting room use

    D. Elections

24. **Which of these is not a reason why schools offer health classes that address issues of sexuality, self-image, peer pressure, nutrition, wellness, gang activity, and drug engagement?**
(Rigorous) (Skill 11.2)

    A. In order to establish a core curriculum that is well-rounded

    B. Because health education is mandated by Title X

    C. To prevent students from engaging in negative activities

    D. So that students are exposed to issues that directly affect them

Case History

Scenario

Tara is a new student in Ms. Fergeson's first grade class. She recently moved to the area from Eastern Europe. She knows very little English but can communicate basic needs. Her parents have a very traditional attitude about school and have told her to obey the teacher and be very quiet in class. Tara was very scared on the first day of school. In her home country, she did not attend school. However, after having been in Ms. Fergeson's class for one month, she is starting to feel more comfortable. She still does not talk much, and she seems very afraid to experiment with creativity. Because she does not talk much, her language skills in English are progressing very slowly. Ms. Fergeson also believes that her unwillingness to communicate will slow her progress in other academic areas, as well.

Ms. Fergeson is a very experienced teacher, but she has rarely had non-native English speakers in her classroom. She has taken courses in language acquisition, but has rarely had the opportunity to witness second language acquisition in progress. Since the first day of school this year, Ms. Fergeson has been very excited to be working with Tara.

A Science Lesson on the Sun, October 20th

Today, students are learning about the sun. Ms. Fergeson has all the students sitting on the floor near an easel (the students are used to calling this part of the room "the carpet"). Ms. Fergeson has manipulatives of the solar system and shows students all the pieces and shares their names. Then, she attaches each piece with velcro to a board on the wall. They are arranged as they would appear in the solar system, with the sun in the middle, and so forth.

Ms. Fergeson pulls out the easel and asks students to share questions with her that they have about the sun. She says that this activity will help them inquire together about the sun. Ms. Fergeson's goal here is to get them to think about what they know and what they do not know about the sun. She is hoping to build a community of curious learners who explore knowledge and apply it to real-life situations. To do this, Ms. Fergeson believes that all students need to be active participants in the learning process. She pushes to have all students share questions and thoughts. Tara sits quietly. Ms. Fergeson asks for her thoughts. Just as Tara is about to say something, the boy next to her quickly and loudly throws his hand in the air to demonstrate to Ms. Fergeson that he has a question. Ms. Fergeson allows him to share his question.

A Reading Lesson, November 10th

The students are sitting back on "the carpet" as Ms. Fergeson introduces the big book they are about to read today. It is an age-appropriate biography of Rosa Parks. Ms. Fergeson wants to start the lesson by teaching the students about genre. She realizes that there are many themes to cover in this book, but she knows that they have not read a biography together yet. She asks students to share types of movies they have seen and types of books they have read. One student responds with the following answer: "I once read a book that was long and had chapters." Ms. Fergeson responded, "No, that is not an example of a genre." Tara, who was about to share that she liked reading funny stories, decided not to share her example.

Ms. Fergeson's Teacher-Reflection Journal, February 2nd

Things seem to be going very well this year. My only concern is Tara. She only thinks concretely about things. I just did not know how to respond when she kept trying to give me factual information when I asked for an opinion. I still don't know what she likes and dislikes; she won't share any opinions of her own. I really wonder if she actually does have any opinions. I am also concerned about the behavior of some of my students. They just do not seem to respond to my rules. My rules are plentiful and extremely specific. The consequences are extremely specific, as well. I just don't know how to get their attention. I've called home numerous times, but nothing has changed. Whenever I can be around them, they behave. But as soon as I turn my back, they're messing around. I also can't get them to get focused when I need them to do so; transitions between activities are taking longer and longer. I had Tara working in a group with other students; I'm really concerned that they were not conducive to her learning today.

Question 1

Ms. Fergeson has noticed that girls in her class, particularly Tara, have a harder time participating in class when boys interrupt.

- What are some of the effects of gender on classroom discussion?
- What can Ms. Fergeson do to promote a fairer, equitable discussion climate in her classroom?

Question 2

Tara is not responsive to Ms. Fergeson's progressive teaching style. Ms. Fergeson asks plenty of questions and really tries to get students to open up with their opinions and observations. Instead, Tara takes everything literally.

- What are possible cultural and cognitive causes of Tara's resistance to being creative and critical?
- What can Ms. Fergeson do to assist Tara in expanding her thinking?

Question 3

Ms. Fergeson realizes that her physical presence to students, her "proximity," reduces misbehaviors. But she does not understand why her rules and consequences, including parent phone calls, do not reduce problems.

- How can Ms. Fergeson use effective verbal and nonverbal communication skills to reduce classroom management problems?

Case History

Franklin Elementary School
Franklin Elementary School is located in an impoverished, mixed racial neighborhood. Its test scores have been declining in recent years. Although the teachers are passionate about what they do and regularly engage in professional development, they are struggling to learn how to teach the rapidly growing second-language population at the school. The school has a new principal who wants to help get teachers more involved in the community and learn more about the expectations of their students' parents. She also wants the teachers to work with data, collaborate more across grade levels, and study new instructional methodologies. While structures for doing such things have been built into the school day, the principal has asked each teacher to outline his or her goals for the school year. The principal will review these with each staff member during performance evaluations.

Mr. Mora
Mr. Mora has been a kindergarten teacher at Franklin for sixteen years. When he began as a teacher, he swore he was going to quickly become a principal. However, the response from the parents of his students was so positive that he felt like he should be in the classroom where he can make the most direct difference with students. Mr. Mora has been an "unofficial" leader at Franklin, though. Many other teachers come to him for advice, and all previous principals have depended upon him to convince staff of important initiatives.

Mr. Mora's "Professional" Goals for the Year
There are six sections on the goals forms; five are for classroom instruction and one addresses professional development. This is what Mr. Mora wrote for the "Professional" section.

I am excited to be working at Franklin for yet another year! I look forward to working with the new principal and helping this school grow. I realize that test scores are going down, but what this school has going for it is positive attitudes. We need to keep that. So, my first goal is to be a positive influence for the rest of the staff. My plan is to maintain a strong demeanor that lets other staff know that Franklin is a great place to work.

My second goal is to work with parents more closely. I have a hard time with this. I feel like my expertise lies in the classroom. I will work harder to communicate with parents and get suggestions from them.

My third goal is to help develop a professional learning community at Franklin that digs deeper into issues of student achievement and works harder to find instructional solutions that work for the entire school.

My fourth goal is to research proven practices to use with my students—and then share those with the rest of the staff. I have a number of activities I constantly do with my students, but I know I can find even better strategies.

My final goal is to work more closely with the resource, reading, and special education teachers. I have tended to close my door and pretend that my classroom is its own world. I need to include all support staff members in the instructional goals of my classroom.

Principal's Mid-Year Assessment of Mr. Mora's Professional Goals

I can definitely say that Mr. Mora is among the most valuable teachers at Franklin Elementary School. Mr. Mora has been a strong voice among staff and has advocated for better instruction, better parental involvement, and a better professional community.

Mr. Mora is definitely moving in the right direction this year in terms of his professional goals. I commend him for maintaining such a positive demeanor! I also commend him for continuing to research best practices. I think he can do more than just go to conferences, though. For professional development, he has tended to miss quite a bit of school.

I do want to suggest a few additional things.

First, while Mr. Mora has involved parents more deeply in his work this year, it has mostly been about student behavior and attendance. He has spent little time trying to figure out how parents can truly be partners in their children's educational experiences.

Second, while it is not Mr. Mora's fault, the professional learning communities that operate at Franklin have tended to be places where teachers complain about their problems with particular students. Again, this is not Mr. Mora's fault, but I sincerely hope that he can work to change that culture of complaining. People look up to him.

Finally, even though Mr. Mora has spent more time working with resource teachers, he has tended to view them as support for *his* instruction. My hope is that he can be more collaborative with them instead.

Overall, though, Mr. Mora is a fantastic teacher and does great things for this school. My job would be much harder were it not for Mr. Mora's dedication and support!

Question 1

Mr. Mora needs to find ways of learning new instructional strategies without attending numerous workshops.

- What other methods of professional development can Mr. Mora engage in to learn additional strategies of enhancing his classroom instruction?
- As a role model for other staff, how can Mr. Mora demonstrate the importance of professional development?

Question 2

Mr. Mora has increased his communication with parents, but he still needs to communicate with them on a deeper level about his students, rather than just calling regarding grades and classroom behavior.

- Discuss the importance of Mr. Mora improving his communication with parents.
- What strategies can Mr. Mora use to improve parental communication?

Question 3

Mr. Mora has spent more time this year working with resource teachers, but his principal believes that more collaboration should take place between Mr. Mora and these teachers.

- What can Mr. Mora do to encourage an attitude of collaboration in his work with the resource teachers?

Praxis Principles of Learning and Teaching (K-6) 0522
Post-Test Sample Questions with Rationales

STUDENTS AS LEARNERS

1. **Which of the following is not a stage in Piaget's theory of child development?**
   (Average) (Skill 1.1)

   A. Sensory motor stage

   B. Pre-optimal stage

   C. Concrete operational

   D. Formal operational

Answer: B. Pre-optimal stage
Jean Piaget, believed children passed through a series of stages to develop from the most basic forms of concrete thinking to sophisticated levels of abstract thinking. His developmental theory consists of four learning stages, which can be remembered with the following pneumonic, Stages Precious Children Follow (SPCF):
   1. Sensory motor stage (from birth to age 2)
   2. Pre-operation stage (ages 2 to 7 or early elementary)
   3. Concrete operational (ages 7 to 11 or upper elementary)
   4. Formal operational (ages 7-15 or late elementary/high school)

2. It is essential that teachers develop relationships with their students and are aware of their personalities. Which of the following is an example of why this is important?
(Easy) (Skill 2.2)

- A. Because most students do not have adult friends
- B. Because most teachers do not have friends who are children
- C. So that teachers can stay abreast of the social interaction between children
- D. Because, then teachers can immediately identify behavioral changes and get the child help

Answer: D. Because, then teachers can immediately identify behavioral changes and get the child help

Social decline is one of the signs of drug or alcohol abuse. In being acquainted with all students, educators will notice personality changes in any student. Characteristically, social withdrawal is first noticed when the student fails to say hello, avoids being near teachers, seems evasive or sneaky, and associates with a different, less academically-focused, group of friends. Obviously, association with known substance abusers is almost always a warning sign. Adults must not accept the explanation that the suspected abusers is just being friends with the known abuser or that the suspected abuser has other kinds of friends. There is a sharp demarcation between youth who abuse substances and those who do not.

3. **When students provide evidence of having special needs, standardized tests can be:**
   (Rigorous) (Skill 2.4)

   A. Given out with the same predetermined questions as what is administered to students without special needs

   B. Exempted for certain children whose special-needs conditions would prevent them performing with any reliability or validity

   C. Administered over a lengthier test period (i.e. 4 hours instead of three or two)

   D. All of the above

Answer: D. All of the above
The intent of testing modifications is to minimize the effect of a student's disability or learning challenge. This provides an equal opportunity for students with disabilities to participate in assessments to demonstrate and express their knowledge and ability. However, if the student's special-needs conditions would prevent them performing with any reliability or validity, they should be exempted from taking the assessment.

4. **Mrs. Grant is providing her students with many extrinsic motivators in order to increase their intrinsic motivation. Which of the following best explains this relationship?**
   (Rigorous) (Skill 3.2)

   A. This is a good relationship and will increase intrinsic motivation

   B. The relationship builds animosity between the teacher and the students

   C. Extrinsic motivation does not in itself help to build intrinsic motivation

   D. There is no place for extrinsic motivation in the classroom

Answer: C. Extrinsic motivation does not in itself help to build intrinsic motivation
There are some cases where it is necessary to utilize extrinsic motivation; however, the use of extrinsic motivation is not typically an effective strategy to build intrinsic motivation. Intrinsic motivation comes from within students themselves, while extrinsic motivation comes from external individuals/forces.

5. **A teacher's posture and movement affect the following student outcomes except:**
   (Easy) (Skill 3.3)

   A. Student learning

   B. Attitudes

   C. Motivation

   D. Physical development

Answer: D. Physical development
Studies show that a teacher's posture and movement are indicators of their enthusiasm and energy, which emphatically influence student outcomes including learning, attitudes, motivation, and focus on goals.

6. **In the classroom, the concept of management transition describes:**
   (Rigorous) (Skill 3.4)

   A. How the administration switches between the principal and vice principal

   B. How parents are prepared for when their children move from one grade to the next

   C. How students monitor the time they spend moving from class to class

   D. How teachers use time effectively so the class moves smoothly from one activity to another

Answer: D. How teachers use time effectively so the class moves smoothly from one activity to another
One way that teachers use class time efficiently is through "management transition", moving smoothly in a systemic, academically oriented way, from one activity to another.

7. **A laminated seating chart can assist teachers in simplifying all of the following tasks except:**
   (Easy) (Skill 3.4)

   A. Performing self-assessments

   B. Taking attendance

   C. Making daily notes

   D. Keeping track of participation

Answer: A. Performing self-assessments
Seating charts can assist teachers in taking attendance; absentees can be spotted in seconds by noting the empty seats, rather than calling each student's name. By laminating the seating chart, the teacher can make daily notes right on the chart. He/she may also efficiently keep track of who is volunteering and who is answering questions. This information can create an equitable classroom climate for all students.

INSTRUCTION AND ASSESSMENT

8. **What is the most important benefit of students developing critical thinking skills?**
   (Easy) (Skill 4.1)

   A. Students are able to apply knowledge to a specific subject area as well as other subject areas

   B. Students remember the information for testing purposes

   C. Students focus on a limited number of specific facts

   D. Students do not have to memorize the information for later recall

Answer: A. Students are able to apply knowledge to a specific subject area as well as other subject areas

When a student learns to think critically, he/she learns how to apply knowledge to a specific subject area; but more importantly, the student knows how to apply that information in other subject areas.

9. **This instructional strategy engages students in active discussion about issues and problems of practical application.**
   (Easy) (Skill 4.2)

   A. Case method

   B. Direct instruction

   C. Concept mapping

   D. Formative assessment

Answer: C. Concept mapping

The case method is an instructional strategy that engages students in active discussion about issues and problems of practical application.

10. Describe the difference between a LAN and a WAN?
    (Average) (Skill 4.4)

    A. WANs allow computers to communicate over greater distances than LANs

    B. LANs allow computers to communicate over greater distances than WANs

    C. WANs and LANs provide the same geographical range

    D. WANs and LANs are both ineffective

Answer: A. WANs allow computers to communicate over greater distances than LANs
With Local Area Networks (LANs), the computers are all contained within the same building or close geographical range. Wide Area Networks (WANs) allow computers to communicate over greater distances.

11. Two powerful internal factors influencing students' academic focus and success are their _____ and _____.
    (Rigorous) (Skill 5.2)

    A. resources and class sizes

    B. parental involvement and teacher preparation

    C. efforts and academic outcomes

    D. attitudes and perceptions about learning

Answer: D. attitudes and perceptions about learning
Students' attitudes and perceptions about learning are two powerful factors influencing academic focus and success. Learners must believe that assigned tasks have some value and that they have the ability and resources to perform them. If a student thinks a task is unimportant, he/she will not put much effort into it.

12. **Which of the following test items is not objective?**
    (Easy) (Skill 6.0)

    A. Multiple choice

    B. Essay

    C. Matching

    D. True/false

Answer: B. Essay
Many forms of assessments are objective such as: multiple choice, yes/no, true/false, and matching. Essays and portfolios on the other hand, are considered open-ended and allow students to provide answers that are more authentic.

13. **Of the following definitions, which best describes a standardized achievement test?**
    (Rigorous) (Skill 6.1)

    A. It measures narrow skills and abilities

    B. It measures broad areas of knowledge

    C. It measures the ability to perform a task

    D. It measures performance related to specific, recently acquired information

Answer: B. It measures broad areas of knowledge
Standardized achievement tests measure a broad scope of content area knowledge. In this way, it may be used on a larger scale in many different states and school districts.

14. It is most appropriate to use norm-referenced standardized tests for which of the following?
    (Average) (Skill 6.1)

    A. For comparison to the population on which the test was normed

    B. For teacher evaluation

    C. For evaluation of the administration

    D. For comparison to school on which the test was normed

Answer: A. For comparison to the population on which the test was normed
While the efficacy of norm-referenced standardized tests have come under attack recently, they are currently the best device for determining where an individual student stands compared to a wide range of peers. They also provide a measure for a program or a school to evaluate how their own students are doing as compared to the populace at large. Even so, they should not be the only measure upon which decisions are made or evaluations drawn. There are many other instruments for measuring student achievement that the teacher needs to consult and take into account.

15. What is the best example of a formative assessment?
    (Average) (Skill 6.2)

    A. The results of an intelligence test

    B. Correcting tests in small groups and immediately recording the grades

    C. An essay that receives teacher feedback and can be corrected by students prior to having a grade recorded

    D. Scheduling a discussion prior to the test

Answer: C. An essay that receives teacher feedback and can be corrected by students prior to having a grade recorded
Formative assessments provide on-going feedback on student progress and the effectiveness of instructional methods and materials. An example is an essay that receives teacher feedback and that can be corrected by students prior to having a grade recorded.

16. This method tests the validity and reliability of a test by dividing a single test into two parts and comparing them.
    (Easy) (Skill 6.3)

    A. Split-half

    B. Test-retest

    C. Equivalent forms

    D. Two-set

Answer: A. Split-half
There are several ways to estimate the reliability of an instrument. The simplest approach is the test-retest method. When the same test is administered again to the same students, if the test is perfectly reliable, each student will receive the same score each time. Even as the scores of individual students vary slightly from one time to the next, it is desirable for the rank order of the students to remain unchanged. Other methods of estimating reliability rely on the same conceptual framework. Split-half methods divide a single test into two parts and compare them. Equivalent forms methods compare two versions of the same test.

17. An example of reliability in testing is ____.
    (Average) (Skill 6.3)

    A. Items on the test produce the same response each time

    B. The test was administered with poor lighting

    C. Items on the test measure what they should measure

    D. The test is too long for the time allotted

Answer: A. Items on the test produce the same response each time
When a test is reliable, it produces the same response each time. A test should give the same results when administered under the same conditions and to the same types of groups of students. This occurs when the items on the test are clear, unambiguous, and not confusing for the students. When items on the test measure what they should measure, this is called validity.

COMMUNICATION TECHNIQUES

18. **Outlines, graphs, and models are particularly good for which type of learners?**
    (Easy) (Skill 7.1)

    A. Auditory

    B. Kinestetic

    C. Visual

    D. Olfactory

Answer: C. Visual
Teachers may choose to use advance organizers that include outlines, graphs, and models. This practice is especially valuable to the visual learner and is a motivational factor for most students.

19. **Which of the following is the best strategy to probe for student understanding of a specific topic?**
    (Rigorous) (Skill 9.1)

    A. Assigning writing exercises that are graded for correctness

    B. Allowing students to write on any topic

    C. Suggesting that students write in a journal that is checked at the end of the semester

    D. Assigning writing exercises that focus on recording students' thoughts on the topic

Answer: D. Assigning writing exercises that focus on recording students' thoughts on the topic
In probing for student understanding of a specific topic, teachers can assign writing exercises that focus not on correctness but on recording students' thoughts on that topic.

PROFESSION AND COMMUNITY

20. Ms. Jones has just read an article on an exciting new instructional strategy; she is considering incorporating this strategy in her classroom. As a research-oriented professional, what should be her next step? *(Rigorous) (Skill 10.2)*

    A. Read textbooks that deal with a wide range of theories

    B. Perform a literature search to see what else has been written on the topic

    C. Talk with other teachers about their opinions

    D. Begin incorporating the strategy with some students in the class

Answer: B. Perform a literature search to see what else has been written on the topic

Good teachers stay on top of what is going on in the field and are constantly looking for ways to improve their teaching. Articles often provide information that can be applied to classroom practices. Research-oriented teachers first read an article more than once carefully to make sure they understanding what is being proposed. Next, they conduct their own literature search to see if they can find where the new theory or approach has been tested and what results have been found. In the case of a debate about a particular theory or practice, they take into account what they have found in their own experience? Just because it is written and published doesn't mean it is true, useful, or applicable to every classroom. Only after the idea passes all of these tests, will experienced teachers incorporate, rate, and evaluate it in their own classrooms.

21. **What is the most powerful benefit of teachers conducting frequent self-assessment?**
    (Average) (Skill 10.3)

    A. They identify areas of weakness and seek professional development opportunities to strengthen them

    B. By observing their own teaching, teachers save themselves the pressure of being observed by others

    C. They also learn their strengths and reduce the time spent on areas not needing attention

    D. Their practice of self-reflection offers a model for students to adopt in self-improvement

Answer: A. They identify areas of weakness and seek professional development opportunities to strengthen them
When a teacher is involved in the process of self-reflection and self-assessment, one of the common outcomes is that the teacher comes to identify areas of skill or knowledge that require more research or improvement on his/her part. He/she may become interested in overcoming a particular weakness by attending a workshop or consulting with a mentor.

22. **Teachers must hold themselves to high standards. When they engage in negative actions such as fighting with students, they are violating all of the following except:**
    (Easy) (Skill 10.3)

    A. Ethics

    B. Professionalism

    C. Morals

    D. Fiscal

Answer: D. Fiscal
Teachers must adhere to strict rules and regulations to maintain the highest degree of conduct and professionalism in the classroom. Current court cases in Florida have examined ethical violations of teachers engaged in improper communication and abuse with students, along with teachers engaged in drug violations and substance abuse in classrooms. It is imperative that today's teachers have the highest regard for professionalism and behave as proper role models for students in and out of the classrooms.

23. Often, schools and communities interact for the following activities except?
 (Average) (Skill 11.1)

    A.   Blood drives

    B.   Legal proceedings

    C.   Meeting room use

    D.   Elections

Answer: B. Legal proceedings
In some places, the community is one entity, the school is another, and rarely do the two meet. Interactions may occur for blood drives and elections. In addition, because the gyms may be the biggest meeting rooms in the city or county, they can be utilized by the larger community.

24. Which of these is not a reason why schools offer health classes that address issues of sexuality, self-image, peer pressure, nutrition, wellness, gang activity, and drug engagement?
 (Rigorous) (Skill 11.2)

    A.   In order to establish a core curriculum that is well-rounded

    B.   Because health education is mandated by Title X

    C.   To prevent students from engaging in negative activities

    D.   So that students are exposed to issues that directly affect them

Answer: B. Because health education is mandated by Title X
Most schools will offer health classes that address issues of sexuality, self-image, peer pressure, nutrition, wellness, gang activity, drug engagement, and a variety of other relevant teen experiences. In most districts, as part of a well-rounded core-curriculum, students are required to take a health class. By setting this mandate, the school and district ensure that students are exposed to issues that directly affect them. In addition, by educating students in such issues, officials seek to prevent students from engaging in negative activities. Even though one health class is rarely enough to effectively address the multiplicity of such issues, in today's era of tight school budgets and financial issues, this is not likely to change.

Answer Key

1. B
2. D
3. D
4. C
5. D
6. D
7. A
8. A
9. C
10. A
11. D
12. B
13. B
14. A
15. C
16. A
17. A
18. C
19. D
20. B
21. A
22. D
23. B
24. B

Rigor Table

	Easy 38%	Average 29%	Rigorous 33%
Questions	2, 5, 7, 8, 9, 12, 16, 18, 22	1, 10, 14, 15, 17, 21, 23	3, 4, 6, 11, 13, 19, 20, 24

Case History

Scenario

Tara is a new student in Ms. Fergeson's first grade class. She recently moved to the area from Eastern Europe. She knows very little English but can communicate basic needs. Her parents have a very traditional attitude about school and have told her to obey the teacher and be very quiet in class. Tara was very scared on the first day of school. In her home country, she did not attend school. However, after having been in Ms. Fergeson's class for one month, she is starting to feel more comfortable. She still does not talk much, and she seems very afraid to experiment with creativity. Because she does not talk much, her language skills in English are progressing very slowly. Ms. Fergeson also believes that her unwillingness to communicate will slow her progress in other academic areas, as well.

Ms. Fergeson is a very experienced teacher, but she has rarely had non-native English speakers in her classroom. She has taken courses in language acquisition, but has rarely had the opportunity to witness second language acquisition in progress. Since the first day of school this year, Ms. Fergeson has been very excited to be working with Tara.

A Science Lesson on the Sun, October 20th

Today, students are learning about the sun. Ms. Fergeson has all the students sitting on the floor near an easel (the students are used to calling this part of the room "the carpet"). Ms. Fergeson has manipulatives of the solar system and shows students all the pieces and shares their names. Then, she attaches each piece with velcro to a board on the wall. They are arranged as they would appear in the solar system, with the sun in the middle, and so forth.

Ms. Fergeson pulls out the easel and asks students to share questions with her that they have about the sun. She says that this activity will help them inquire together about the sun. Ms. Fergeson's goal here is to get them to think about what they know and what they do not know about the sun. She is hoping to build a community of curious learners who explore knowledge and apply it to real-life situations. To do this, Ms. Fergeson believes that all students need to be active participants in the learning process. She pushes to have all students share questions and thoughts. Tara sits quietly. Ms. Fergeson asks for her thoughts. Just as Tara is about to say something, the boy next to her quickly and loudly throws his hand in the air to demonstrate to Ms. Fergeson that he has a question. Ms. Fergeson allows him to share his question.

A Reading Lesson, November 10th
The students are sitting back on "the carpet" as Ms. Fergeson introduces the big book they are about to read today. It is an age-appropriate biography of Rosa Parks. Ms. Fergeson wants to start the lesson by teaching the students about genre. She realizes that there are many themes to cover in this book, but she knows that they have not read a biography together yet. She asks students to share types of movies they have seen and types of books they have read. One student responds with the following answer: "I once read a book that was long and had chapters." Ms. Fergeson responded, "No, that is not an example of a genre." Tara, who was about to share that she liked reading funny stories, decided not to share her example.

Ms. Fergeson's Teacher-Reflection Journal, February 2nd
Things seem to be going very well this year. My only concern is Tara. She only thinks concretely about things. I just did not know how to respond when she kept trying to give me factual information when I asked for an opinion. I still don't know what she likes and dislikes; she won't share any opinions of her own. I really wonder if she actually does have any opinions. I am also concerned about the behavior of some of my students. They just do not seem to respond to my rules. My rules are plentiful and extremely specific. The consequences are extremely specific, as well. I just don't know how to get their attention. I've called home numerous times, but nothing has changed. Whenever I can be around them, they behave. But as soon as I turn my back, they're messing around. I also can't get them to get focused when I need them to do so; transitions between activities are taking longer and longer. I had Tara working in a group with other students; I'm really concerned that they were not conducive to her learning today.

Question 1

Ms. Fergeson has noticed that girls in her class, particularly Tara, have a harder time participating in class when boys interrupt.

- What are some of the effects of gender on classroom discussion?
- What can Ms. Fergeson do to promote a fairer, equitable discussion-climate in her classroom?

Sample Answer

Tara's experience during the science lesson is not rare. Gender differences are not universal, and it is not appropriate to apply firm labels to either girls or boys. However, research has shown that in spite of movements towards teaching both genders equitably, there is still much room for progress. For instance, in Ms. Ferguson's class, it is likely that other girls have been able to participate as much as they could, but gender differences still factor into the class participation. There are a few reasons for this.

First, many boys are taught by parents and older siblings to be assertive, while many girls are taught to be passive. Second, boys tend to be hyper, and many have trouble sitting still. By participating frequently, they appropriately direct their energy to classroom learning. This is a good thing for boys. Unfortunately, many girls get shut out of the conversations, unless they are assertive, as well. Indeed, many shy boys do not participate because they are overshadowed by their more assertive classmates. While boys and girls have different tendencies and inclinations in classroom situations, they can also be taught how to behave appropriately.

Ms. Fergeson should consider her teaching of discussion skills to be an on-going, context-based process. It is simply not enough to provide children with rules. At the first grade level, their social development is still very basic, and they will need to have constant reminders in the form of modeling, suggestions, and hints. A classroom climate of respect must be established, and Ms. Fergeson will have to remind students of the characteristics of respect on a regular basis. She can also institute various fun ways of distributing participation in class. For example, she can use popsicle sticks with students' names on them as a way to randomly choose students to participate. She can also let everyone know that each person has to come up with one thing to say—and then go around in a circle and have everyone present. Another strategy is to have students share thoughts to a partner so that everyone participates in a short amount of time.

Commentary on Sample Answer
This essay would receive a 2 as it responds to all parts of the question, provides multiple details, and references aspects of gender and communication appropriate to the case.

Question 2

Tara is not responsive to Ms. Fergeson's progressive teaching style. Ms. Fergeson asks plenty of questions and really tries to get students to open up with their opinions and observations. Instead, Tara takes everything literally.

- What are possible cultural and cognitive causes of Tara's resistance to being creative and critical?
- What can Ms. Fergeson do to assist Tara in expanding her thinking?

Sample Answer

Tara is unresponsive to Ms. Fergeson's teaching first and foremost because of the cultural differences that exist between her family and American classroom culture. Even though she knows she is safe to share opinions in class, she has the fear that her parents will find out. She realizes that her parents will not understand that this is acceptable in American classrooms. She may also want to avoid any confrontations between Ms. Fergeson and her parents.

In addition, not all children are cognitively capable of thinking beyond concrete concepts. Often, it takes children a few additional years to fully develop critical thinking skills. Perhaps Tara is not yet at the level Ms. Fergeson thinks she should be. Ms. Fergeson may want to re-asses her understanding of cognitive stages of children. In spite of this, Ms. Fergeson can still promote creative thinking in Tara by giving her smaller steps by which to practice. For example, the instance in the reading lesson where the other student was firmly told "No" in regard to the answer offered may have scared Tara into thinking that her answer may be incorrect. Undoubtedly, she may not have wanted to risk getting a "wrong" answer. Ms. Fergeson could have taken that incorrect answer and questioned the student further until an appropriate answer was offered. Additionally, Ms. Fergeson could work individually with Tara to ask her questions to help her open up in a more personal setting. Then, Tara could move up to discussions in small groups.

Commentary on Sample Answer

This answer would receive a 2. It successfully ties cognitive and cultural theories to practical student situations and classroom teaching advice.

Question 3

Ms. Fergeson realizes that her physical presence to students, her "proximity", reduces misbehaviors. But she does not understand why her rules and consequences, including parent phone calls, do not reduce problems.

- How can Ms. Fergeson use effective verbal and nonverbal communication skills to reduce classroom management problems?

Sample Answer

Ms. Fergeson obviously cannot be in all places at all times. She has to set up a very simple, structured set of behavior expectations, stick to them, and always be noticeable throughout the entire classroom and class period. Complicated rules and consequences are confusing to young students. Not only are intricate rules developmentally inappropriate for first graders, they often result in students not remembering the few most important aspects of classroom citizenship. Another consideration is that classroom design is an important factor in nonverbal communication. In classrooms where the teacher cannot always see all students, such as when desks are arranged in rows, students feel less "pressure" from the teacher. It is almost like the teacher is not there.

Ms. Fergeson can be more visible, though, if she were to design her room so that she can give regular glances to those talkative students. In designing transitions between lessons and activities, teachers can develop routines that all students must follow. For example, Ms. Fergeson might flash the lights once, and all students would be required to "freeze" and wait for instructions from Ms. Fergeson. Creative teachers can make games out of this. For example, Ms. Fergeson might add up all the time it takes for students to transition and challenge students to keep their minutes of "non-instructional time" under a certain amount for an appropriate time period. For first graders, this may be for one-week periods. Finally, when Ms. Fergeson places students, such as Tara, around regularly problematic students, she should maintain a stronger proximal presence.

Commentary on Sample Answer

This answer would receive a 2. It effectively answers the question in a theoretical sense and provides numerous classroom strategies for Ms. Fergeson to try.

Case History

Franklin Elementary School

Franklin Elementary School is located in an impoverished, mixed racial neighborhood. Its test scores have been declining in recent years. Although the teachers are passionate about what they do and regularly engage in professional development, they are struggling to learn how to teach the rapidly growing second-language population at the school. The school has a new principal who wants to help get teachers more involved in the community and learn more about the expectations of their students' parents. She also wants the teachers to work with data, collaborate more across grade levels, and study new instructional methodologies. While structures for doing such things have been built into the school day, the principal has asked each teacher to outline his or her goals for the school year. The principal will review these with each staff member during performance evaluations.

Mr. Mora

Mr. Mora has been a kindergarten teacher at Franklin for sixteen years. When he began as a teacher, he swore he was going to quickly become a principal. However, the response from the parents of his students was so positive that he felt like he should be in the classroom where he can make the most direct difference with students. Mr. Mora has been an "unofficial" leader at Franklin, though. Many other teachers come to him for advice, and all previous principals have depended upon him to convince staff of important initiatives.

Mr. Mora's "Professional" Goals for the Year

There are six sections on the goals forms; five are for classroom instruction and one addresses professional development. This is what Mr. Mora wrote for the "Professional" section.

I am excited to be working at Franklin for yet another year! I look forward to working with the new principal and helping this school grow. I realize that test scores are going down, but what this school has going for it is positive attitudes. We need to keep that. So, my first goal is to be a positive influence for the rest of the staff. My plan is to maintain a strong demeanor that lets other staff know that Franklin is a great place to work.

My second goal is to work with parents more closely. I have a hard time with this. I feel like my expertise lies in the classroom. I will work harder to communicate with parents and get suggestions from them.

My third goal is to help develop a professional learning community at Franklin that digs deeper into issues of student achievement and works harder to find instructional solutions that work for the entire school.

My fourth goal is to research proven practices to use with my students—and then share those with the rest of the staff. I have a number of activities I constantly do with my students, but I know I can find even better strategies.

My final goal is to work more closely with the resource, reading, and special education teachers. I have tended to close my door and pretend that my classroom is its own world. I need to include all support staff members in the instructional goals of my classroom.

Principal's Mid-Year Assessment of Mr. Mora's Professional Goals

I can definitely say that Mr. Mora is among the most valuable teachers at Franklin Elementary School. Mr. Mora has been a strong voice among staff and has advocated for better instruction, better parental involvement, and a better professional community.

Mr. Mora is definitely moving in the right direction this year in terms of his professional goals. I commend him for maintaining such a positive demeanor! I also commend him for continuing to research best practices. I think he can do more than just go to conferences, though. For professional development, he has tended to miss quite a bit of school.

I do want to suggest a few additional things.

First, while Mr. Mora has involved parents more deeply in his work this year, it has mostly been about student behavior and attendance. He has spent little time trying to figure out how parents can truly be partners in their children's educational experiences.

Second, while it is not Mr. Mora's fault, the professional learning communities that operate at Franklin have tended to be places where teachers complain about their problems with particular students. Again, this is not Mr. Mora's fault, but I sincerely hope that he can work to change that culture of complaining. People look up to him.

Finally, even though Mr. Mora has spent more time working with resource teachers, he has tended to view them as support for *his* instruction. My hope is that he can be more collaborative with them instead.

Overall, though, Mr. Mora is a fantastic teacher and does great things for this school. My job would be much harder were it not for Mr. Mora's dedication and support!

Question 1

Mr. Mora needs to find ways of learning new instructional strategies without attending numerous workshops.

- What other methods of professional development can Mr. Mora engage in to learn additional strategies of enhancing his classroom instruction?
- As a role model for other staff, how can Mr. Mora demonstrate the importance of professional development?

Sample Answer

One thing Mr. Mora's principal hoped was that Mr. Mora would be a stronger influence on the culture of the staff. Mr. Mora can be a strong encourager of faculty study groups, lesson study groups, student work analysis sessions, and other activities that promote teacher learning in a collective sense. While there is no substitute for learning new strategies from professional, research-based sources (journal articles, workshop presentations, etc.), this is not feasible for most teachers. Just as powerful, though, is situated teacher learning, where teachers learn in the contexts of their own schools.

The school already has professional learning communities; therefore, Mr. Mora can encourage these communities to engage in activities that promote teacher learning about the techniques that will help their students succeed. For example, Mr. Mora can investigate methods of engaging in lesson study, a technique used in Japan to analyze the quality of lessons. Doing this allows staff to talk about strategies they have seen work and then investigate reasons why other strategies may not work so well. Mr. Mora can be a voice for the importance of professional development by demonstrating, as a sixteen-year veteran, that improvement in instruction never ends. By showing that he constantly wants to improve, he will hopefully inspire other, younger teachers and show that teacher learning does not end with college, nor does it reside only in workshops and conferences.

Commentary on Sample Answer

This answer would earn a score of 2 as it provides a theoretical foundation for teacher learning in communities, and it provides specific recommendations for Mr. Mora.

Question 2

Mr. Mora has increased his communication with parents, but he still needs to communicate with them on a deeper level about his students, rather than just calling regarding grades and classroom behavior.

- Discuss the importance of Mr. Mora improving his communication with parents.
- What strategies can Mr. Mora use to improve parental communication?

Sample Answer

Many parents do not know how to respond to teachers' requests to communicate or participate. In many cultures, teachers are treated as the main source and authority on student learning. In the United States, teachers are seen as partners with parents to encourage intellectual and emotional growth in children. To get to the point where partnership is realized, though, requires that teachers work with parents, rather than just calling to inform them about problems, such as behavioral incidents.

For example, teachers and parents can discuss classroom and learning goals for the year; they can ask parents for feedback on their work as a teacher or for advice on dealing with students. Many parents are afraid that their only interactions with teachers will be negative. By opening the conversation up to be informational, positive, and two-sided, Mr. Mora can encourage parents be more honest and forthright. And in the process, he will undoubtedly help the parents to be more comfortable at the school. In addition to these types of meetings, Mr. Mora can make arrangements to have meetings with the parents at students' homes. That way, he will begin to understand his students' cultures in greater depth.

Commentary on Sample Answer

This response would earn a score of 2, as it thoroughly answers the questions with multiple strategies connected to theories of parental communication.

Question 3

Mr. Mora has spent more time this year working with resource teachers, but his principal believes that more collaboration should take place between Mr. Mora and these teachers.

- What can Mr. Mora do to encourage an attitude of collaboration in his work with the resource teachers?

Sample Answer

Too often, teachers view their classrooms as isolated places of student learning—unconnected to the rest of the school. However, all effective teachers recognize that they cannot single-handedly deal with all student concerns each day. They need support from other professionals who can work with specific needs. And while general teachers' plans may meet the needs of some or most students, they do not always meet all students' needs. Therefore, instead of simply having resource teachers tailor their work to meet the needs of the general teacher, all students will benefit from the collaborative approach of multiple teachers working together.

Indeed, even average or gifted students can benefit from the instructional approaches of reading specialists and special education teachers. These teachers often have very unique techniques that can enhance the learning of all students. In the research on teacher collaboration, we find that interdependence between teachers is stronger than other types of collective work, including help-seeking and "pull-out" methods. Therefore, Mr. Mora might consider scheduling some time each week to discuss instructional plans, student work, and classroom modifications with the resource teachers. He can come to these meetings with a rough plan on what he wants to accomplish in the week; then, after discussing ideas with the resource teachers, he can develop specific plans.

Commentary on Sample Answer

This answer would receive a score of 2 as it draws upon research and theory of teacher collaboration and provides a specific example of how Mr. Mora can apply that research to his own work.

www.ingramcontent.com/pod-product-compliance
Lightning Source LLC
LaVergne TN
LVHW061320060426
835507LV00019B/2242

9781607871309